D1709974

The Countries

Portugal

Bob Italia

ABDO Publishing Company

visit us at
www.abdopub.com

Published by ABDO Publishing Company, 4940 Viking Drive, Edina, Minnesota 55435.
Copyright © 2002 by Abdo Consulting Group, Inc. International copyrights reserved in
all countries. No part of this book may be reproduced in any form without written
permission from the publisher.

Printed in the United States.

Photo Credits: Corbis
Art Direction & Maps: Neil Klinepier

Library of Congress Cataloging-in-Publication Data

Italia, Bob, 1955-
    Portugal / Bob Italia.
      p. cm. -- (The countries)
    Includes index.
    Summary: Provides an overview of the history, geography, people, economy, holidays,
and other aspects of life in Portugal.
    ISBN 1-57765-758-6
     1. Portugal--Juvenile literature. [1. Portugal.] I. Title. II. Series.

DP517 .I73 2002
946.9--dc21

                                        2001045851

Contents

Alô!

Hello from Portugal, the westernmost country of continental Europe.

Portuguese explorers began the great age of European exploration. The Portuguese empire weakened in the late 1500s, but did not end until the 1900s. Today, Portugal is a **republic** with elected government officials.

Portugal has four main land regions and a mild climate. Over the years, people have hurt its plant life. And the variety of wildlife in Portugal is small.

The main **ethnic** group of the country is Portuguese. Portuguese is the official language. Roman Catholicism is the most practiced religion. Religion plays an important role in Portugal's holiday seasons.

Most Portuguese live in **rural** villages and work as farmers. But the cities and their **industries** are growing rapidly. Cotton fabric and other **textiles** are Portugal's main manufactured products.

Portugal has extensive railroad and highway systems that connect most cities and towns. The national government owns Portugal's telephone, telegraph, and postal systems.

Portuguese people enjoy recreational activities such as folk songs, bullfights, and soccer. They also have a rich history of arts and crafts. And the country is well-known for its churches and monuments built long ago.

Alô *from Portugal!*

Fast Facts

LISBON

OFFICIAL NAME: Republica Portuguesa (Portuguese
Republic)
CAPITAL: Lisbon

LAND
- Mountain Range: Serra da Estrela
- Highest Peak: *Malhão da Estrela* 6,539 feet (1,993 m)
- Major Rivers: Douro, Tagus, Guadiana

PEOPLE
- Population: 9,863,000 (2002 est.)
- Major Cities: Lisbon, Porto
- Language: Portuguese
- Religions: Roman Catholicism, Protestantism, Islam,
Judaism

GOVERNMENT
- Form: Parliamentary democracy
- Chief of State: President
- Chief of Government: Prime minister
- Legislature: Parliament
- National Anthem: "A Portuguesa" ("The Portuguese")

ECONOMY
- Agricultural Products: Grapes, tomatoes, potatoes, corn;
hogs, chickens, milk, beef cattle
- Manufactured Products: Textiles, food products, paper
products, electrical machinery, cork products, ceramics,
shoes, cement, fertilizer
- Fishing: Sardines, tuna
- Mining Products: Marble, coal, copper, wolframite
- Money: Escudo and euro (100 centavos = 1 escudo, 100
cents = 1 euro)

Portugal's flag

Portugal's escudo

Timeline

3000 B.C.	Iberians settle in Portugal
A.D. 476	Visigoths conquer the Iberian Peninsula
early 700s	North African Muslims seize control of Portugal
1143	Alfonso Henriques becomes king of Portugal
1385	King John I comes to power
mid-1500s	Portuguese empire reaches its peak
1580	Spain conquers Portugal
1640	Duke of Braganza reclaims Portugal's independence
1908	King Carlos I and his eldest son are assassinated
1910	Portugal becomes a republic
1914 to 1918	Portugal helps the Allies during World War I
1926	Antonio de Oliveira Salazar becomes dictator
1968	Marcello Caetano becomes dictator
1974	Portugal abolishes dictatorship
1976	Portugal adopts a new constitution and becomes a parliamentary democracy
1986	Mário Soares becomes president
1996	Jorge Sampaio becomes president
2001	Jorge Sampaio wins re-election

History

Prehistoric people lived in present-day Portugal more than 100,000 years ago. About 5,000 years ago, people known as Iberians settled the Iberian Peninsula.

In 201 B.C., the Romans gained control of the Iberian Peninsula. But then in A.D. 476, the Visigoths, a Christian Germanic tribe, conquered the peninsula.

A Visigoth king and his soldiers

In the early 700s, North African Muslims seized control of Portugal. Iberian Christians were against Muslim rule. They fought the Muslims for hundreds of years.

In 1094, Alfonso VI, the Christian king of Spain, gave Henry of Burgundy, a French nobleman, land rights to northern Portugal. The king considered Portugal to be a part of Spain.

Henry of Burgundy's son, Alfonso Henriques, won many battles against the Muslims. In 1143, he became king of Portugal, and the country became independent.

In 1385, King John I came to power. His armies defeated Spanish forces trying to conquer Portugal.

Portugal soon became a seafaring power. Portuguese sailors reached the Madeira Islands in 1419, and the Azores in 1431. In 1498, Portuguese explorer Vasco da Gama reached India. In 1500, he arrived in Brazil. By the mid-1500s, Portugal's empire stretched from Africa to Brazil, Malaysia, Indonesia, and China.

King Carlos I

Spain conquered Portugal in 1580. But in 1640, the Duke of Braganza reclaimed Portugal's independence. He became King John IV. Portugal's new empire lasted into the 1900s.

In 1908, King Carlos I and his eldest son were **assassinated** by **revolutionaries**. The king's son, Manuel II, became king. But in 1910, revolutionaries forced him from the throne. Portugal became a **republic**.

The new republic had many problems. Portugal had 45 different governments in just 15 years. During World War I (1914-1918), Portugal helped the **Allies** fight the **Central Powers**. But the war hurt its weak **economy**.

In 1926, Portugal's army took control of the government. Antonio de Oliveira Salazar, a government minister, became **dictator**. Then in 1932, he was named **prime minister**.

Antonio de Oliveira Salazar

Salazar held power for decades. But in the 1960s, he encountered trouble. In 1961, Portugal lost its last colony in India. In 1968, Salazar suffered a stroke. Marcello Caetano became Portugal's **dictator**. He ruled until 1974.

In 1975, the **Constituent Assembly** wrote a new **constitution**. In April 1976, the new constitution was approved. Portugal became a **parliamentary democracy**. Voters elected a new president, António Ramalho Eanes, and a new **parliament**. Mário Soares became **prime minister**.

From 1976 to 1985, Portugal had many political problems and different leaders. In 1986, Mário Soares became president. He won another term in 1991.

In 1995, António Guterres became prime minister. The next year, Jorge Sampaio became president. He won re-election in 2001.

Jorge Sampaio

The Land

Portugal has four main land regions: the Coastal Plains, the Northern Tablelands, the Central Range, and the Southern Tablelands.

The Coastal Plains region is mostly flatlands used for farming. The Northern Tablelands, Central Range, and Southern Tablelands have plains and mountain ranges.

The Central Range region has Portugal's highest mountains, the Serra da Estrela range. Portugal's highest mountain, *Malhão da Estrela*, is located here.

Portugal has three major rivers, the Douro, the Tagus, and the Guadiana. The Douro and the Tagus flow west into the Atlantic Ocean. The Guadiana forms part of the boundary with Spain.

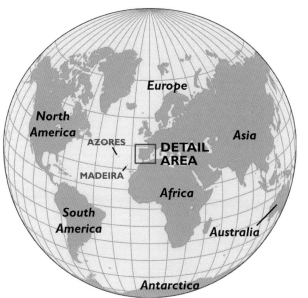

Because it is on the Atlantic Ocean, Portugal has a mild climate. Portugal has warm and dry summers. Winters are cool with heavy rains. A little snow falls in the north, and covers the highest peaks of the Serra da Estrela range.

The Serra da Estrela mountain range

Rainfall

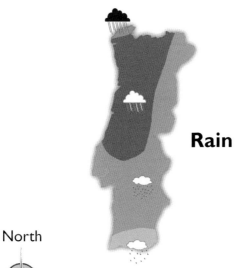

Rain

AVERAGE YEARLY RAINFALL

Inches		Centimeters
Under 20		Under 50
20 - 40		50 - 100
40 - 60		100 - 150
Over 60		Over 150

North

West — East

South

Temperature

Summer

AVERAGE TEMPERATURE

Fahrenheit		Celsius
Over 76°		Over 24°
65° - 76°		18° - 24°
54° - 65°		12° - 18°
43° - 54°		6° - 12°
32° - 43°		0° - 6°

Winter

Plants & Animals

Human activity in Portugal has hurt its plant life. The thickest forests are found in the north, where oak, pine, cork oak, chestnut, and eucalyptus grow. Olive trees grow well inland. In the Douro valley, juniper scrub has been mostly cleared for vineyards. In the warmer climates of the south, there are olive, vine, fig, almond, and carob trees.

The cork oak

Monk seals

The variety of wildlife in Portugal is small. Portugal has a mix of European and North African animals. Wild goat, wild pig, and deer are found in the countryside. The wolf is found in the Serra da Estrela, and the lynx in south-central Portugal. The fox, rabbit, and Iberian hare are common everywhere.

The Azores have smaller mammals such as rabbits, weasels, ferrets, rats, mice, and bats. Monk seals are found on the Madeira Islands. And many kinds of fish are found in the Atlantic Ocean, especially the European sardine.

The Portuguese

The main **ethnic** group of the country is Portuguese. The only main **minority** group is Africans from Portugal's former African colonies. The Portuguese can trace their roots to the many different peoples who settled or conquered the land. These have included Celts, Phoenicians, Carthaginians, Romans, Jews, Germanic tribes, Arabs, and Berbers.

Portuguese is the official language. It is very similar to Spanish. Most Portuguese are Roman Catholics. There are also small groups of Jews, Muslims, and Protestants.

Most Portuguese live in small homes in small, coastal fishing or farm villages. But the cities are growing rapidly, as Portugal's growing **industries** create more jobs. Most people live in apartment buildings or small, white-washed houses. But **shantytowns** have developed on the edges of the cities. **Villas** are sometimes found in the countryside. It is common for three generations of one family to live in the same house.

Most Portuguese wear Western European-style clothing. But in some **rural** areas, people wear traditional clothes. Alentejo cattlemen still wear red and green stocking caps. The *samarra*, a short jacket with a fur collar, and *cifões,* or **chaps**, are worn also. Some shepherds wear straw cloaks.

Single-story houses line a sloped street in the town of Alcacovas.

Beef, pork, chicken, beans, rice, fresh fruit, and potatoes are popular foods. Olive oil, eggs, and herbs are common ingredients. A favorite Portuguese dish is steak with french fried potatoes, and an egg on top. In northern Portugal and along the coast, cod and sardines are popular. Bread is made of maize, rye, or wheat. Wine and coffee are popular beverages.

Portugal does not have a solid education system. Portuguese children must attend school between the ages of 6 and 15. But many parts of the country have no high schools. And most adults cannot read or write.

A Portuguese dish of grilled sardines

Fillozes
Portuguese Donuts

3 cups flour
1/2 tsp salt
1 yeast cake

1 cup butter
3 tbsp sugar

1 cup oil
9 eggs

Dissolve yeast in 1/4 cup lukewarm water. Beat eggs well, add sugar, beat well, add dissolved yeast. Mix with flour and work together until it forms a soft dough, beating well. Melt butter and let cool to lukewarm, then pour into dough, work together well, and set in warm place to rise until it doubles in size. Heat oil to boiling on low heat. Put milk in saucer, dip hands in milk. Take dough (1 tbsp) in hand. Keep stretching until round and thin. Drop piece into oil, turning as needed to brown on both sides. Coat each one in sugar while still warm.

AN IMPORTANT NOTE TO THE CHEF: Always have an adult help with the preparation and cooking of food. Never use kitchen utensils or appliances without adult permission and supervision.

English	Portuguese
Yes	Bem
No	Não
Thank You	Obrigado
Please	Faça favor
Hello	Alô
Goodbye	Adeus

LANGUAGE

The Economy

Cotton fabric and other **textiles** are Portugal's main manufactured products. Other important manufactured products include food products, paper products, and electrical machinery. Portugal's food-processing **industries** include meat packing, animal feed production, canned sardines, and wine. Portuguese factories also make cement, ceramics, cork products, shoes, and fertilizer.

Most Portuguese work in agriculture. Most farmers own small farms and use old-fashioned equipment. But there are large, state-owned collective farms that use modern methods and machines.

Wine grapes are an important agricultural product. Other crops include almonds, corn, olives, potatoes, rice, tomatoes, and wheat. Cattle, chickens, hogs, and sheep are also raised.

Portugal has some valuable natural resources. In coastal fishing villages, cod, sardines, tuna, and many other kinds of fish are caught. But mineral resources have not been developed well. The most important mineral is decorative marble, which is **quarried**. Portugal also has coal, copper, and wolframite deposits. And cork oak trees in central and southern Portugal are harvested for their cork.

A marble quarry in Estremos

Cities

Portugal has two main cities, Lisbon and Porto. Lisbon is Portugal's capital and largest city. It is also the country's **economic**, political, and **cultural** center.

Lisbon has many public squares, statues, tree-lined streets, and small parks. Portugal's national library is there. The Sao Carlos Opera House, the Tower of Belém, and the Castle of Sao Jorge are popular tourist sites.

Lisbon is also Portugal's main port. Ceramics, cork, sardines, tomato paste, and wine are exported from its harbor. The city is home to Portugal's chief banks, insurance companies, and investment firms. It also has an international airport. People move about the city in buses, electric trains, streetcars, and a subway system.

Porto is Portugal's second-largest city and **economic** center of the north. Porto processes and exports Portugal's famous port wines. The city also has food-processing plants, sugar **refineries**, and **textile** mills. Tourist attractions include the cathedral and the bishop's palace.

A view of Lisbon

Transportation & Communication

Portugal has an extensive government-owned railroad system that connects most cities and towns. Trains, streetcars, and subways transport people in the cities.

Portugal's government also owns the national airline, *Transportes Aéreos Portugueses* (TAP), or Air Portugal. Lisbon Airport is the main international airport.

Most Portuguese do not own automobiles. Still, Portugal has a good highway system. A four-lane *auto-estrada,* or superhighway, connects Lisbon to Porto. Other highways connect Porto and Lisbon to Spain. Highways also connect other towns. Secondary roads connect most towns. In **rural** areas, some people still travel by oxcart, horse, or mule.

The national government owns Portugal's telephone, telegraph, and postal systems. There are more radios than televisions in Portugal. Portugal has about 25 daily newspapers.

A streetcar in Lisbon

Government

Portugal is a **republic**. It has a president, a **prime minister**, and a **parliament**.

The president is the head of state. He or she appoints a prime minister. The people elect the president to a five-year term.

The prime minister heads the government. The prime minister chooses **cabinet** members to help run the government.

The parliament is called the Assembly of the Republic. It makes Portugal's laws. The 230 assembly members are elected by the people and serve four-year terms.

Portugal is divided into 22 local government districts. Each district elects a governor and **legislature** to run the district government.

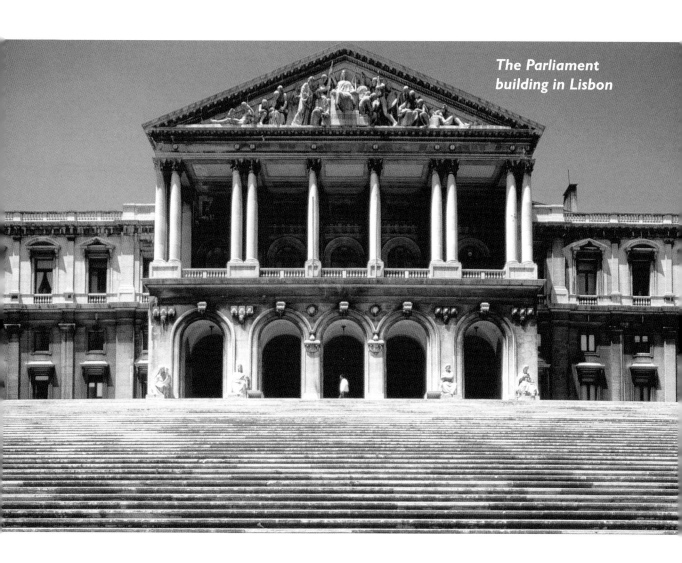

The Parliament building in Lisbon

Holidays & Festivals

Religion plays an important part in Portugal's holiday seasons. Portugal has many religious **pilgrimages**, festivals, fairs, and processions. During the Christmas season, yule logs are burned in village churches, so that the poor may warm themselves.

Domingo de Ramos is celebrated the Sunday before Easter. It honors the 40 days Jesus spent praying on Olivetrees Hill. Participants gather olivetree branches and rosemary, then go to church in procession.

Each year, thousands of people make a pilgrimage to the Portuguese town of Fatima. There, in 1917, the Virgin Mary appeared to three children. The Basilica of Our Lady of Fatima stands on the site.

Carnival is one of Portugal's biggest events. It takes place about six weeks before Easter. People paint their faces and go to parties and parades.

The *Festa de São João* in June is biggest in Porto. The festival honors St. John, and lasts several days. It includes bullfights, dances, and a parade of **antiques**.

The *25 de Abril* celebrates the day in 1974 when the Portuguese people received their freedom from **dictatorial** rule.

Guitarists play and walk the streets of Angra do Heroismo during the Festa de São João.

Sports & Leisure

Portuguese people enjoy recreational activities such as folk songs, bullfights, and soccer.

The Portuguese have lively folk songs called *chulas* and *vira*. A guitar is used when singing sad songs called *fados*.

Bullfighting is famous and popular in Portugal and Spain. But in Portugal, the bullfighter sometimes rides a horse and is not allowed to kill the bull. The bull's horns are often covered to protect the horse.

A Portuguese bullfight

The Portuguese national soccer cup final in Lisbon

Soccer is the most popular team sport in Portugal. It is played in all parts of the country, and attracts the most spectators. Basketball and roller hockey are other popular team sports. The Portuguese also like to spend time on the beautiful beaches along their country's long seacoast.

Portugal is well-known for its many beautiful churches. Artists decorated them with religious paintings and sculptures.

Lisbon has popular monuments, including the *Mosteiro dos Jerónimos* and the *Torre de Belém*. Lisbon's museums include the *Museu Nacional do Azulejo*, and the *Museu Nacional de Arte Antiga*, which displays the works of Portuguese painters. Another museum, the *Museu*

The Tower of Belém was built in 1515 to protect the entrance of the Tagus River.

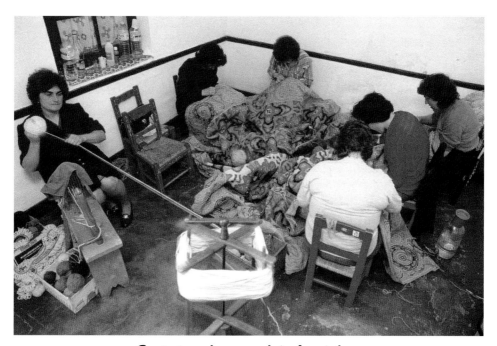

Carpet makers work in Arraiolos.

Calouste Gulbenkian, has paintings, sculptures, carpets, coins, and ceramics from all over the world.

The Portuguese are proud of their craftwork. Their pottery, lace, embroidery, carpets, and linen are world famous.

The Portuguese have a long history of fine literary works. In 1998, the Portuguese novelist José Saramago won the Nobel Prize for literature.

Glossary

allies - countries that agree to help each other in times of need. During World War I, the Allies fought the Central Powers. The Allies were made up of more than twenty countries, including Great Britain, France, and the United States.

antique - an old item that has collectible value.

assassinate - to murder an important person.

cabinet - a group of advisers chosen by the prime minister to lead government departments.

Central Powers - During World War I, Germany, Bulgaria, Austria, and the Ottoman Empire were called the Central Powers. They fought the Allies.

chaps - leather flaps worn over pant legs and joined by a belt.

Constituent Assembly - a group of people in Portugal's government who represented all the people.

constitution - the laws that govern a country.

culture - the customs, arts, and tools of a nation or people at a certain time.

dictator - a ruler who has complete control and usually governs in a cruel or unfair way.

economy - the way a nation uses its money, goods, and natural resources.

ethnic - a way to describe a group of people who have the same race, nationality, or culture.

industry - all of a country's manufacturing plants, businesses, and trade.

legislative - the branch of a government that makes laws.

minority - a racial, religious, or political group that is different from the larger group of which it is a part.

parliament - the highest lawmaking body of some governments.

parliamentary democracy - a form of government in which the decisions of the nation are made by the people, through the elected body of parliament.

pilgrimage - a journey to a holy place.

prime minister - the highest-ranked member of some governments.

quarry - a place where stone, slate, or limestone is mined.

refinery - the building and machinery for purifying sugar, petroleum, and other things.

republic - a form of government in which authority rests with voting citizens and is carried out by elected officials such as a parliament.

revolutionary - a person who tries to cause a sudden and complete change in government.

rural - of or related to the countryside.

shantytown - an area of small, poorly built homes.

textile - of or having to do with the designing, manufacturing, or producing of woven fabric.

villa - a large, expensive house located in the country, on the edge of a city, or at the seashore.

Web Sites

The Portuguese Republic
http://www.presidenciarepublica.pt/en/main.html
This is the official site of the Portuguese Republic and president. Readers can learn about Portugal, its current president, and see where the president lives.

Portuguese Explorers
http://lcweb.loc.gov/rr/hispanic/portam/role.html
This Library of Congress site has information on Portugal and the Age of Discovery. Find out details about the main Portuguese voyages, and see how they saw the world in the seventeenth century.

These sites are subject to change. Go to your favorite search engine and type in Portugal for more sites.

Index